Petty

noun

1. 1. (of behavior) characterized by an undue concern for trivial matters, especially in a small-minded or spiteful way.

Cache

2. a collection of items of the same type stored in a hidden or inaccessible place.

Yes, I am very petty.

But only when its necessary,

Of course.

-Assata Akil

Table of Contents

February Blues

Love came fast then

love went quick.

It made me feel good

Now I'm feeling sick

I gave up my wings

My ticket to be free

Only to realize that I was in love

with a love

That didn't have love for me.

Love Poem for Losers

Love is for Loserssssss

Unless, you're a chooser

Though I choose to chose wrong,

I still love a good love song

I declare it's true; Love is for Losers!

Refute! Turn into Refusers.

Unless you love a good tale

Just have your money to make bail

Because love may be your cell.

I will say this; Love is a game

for those whom are willing

To lose.

Who is worth the loss?

I'm afraid you will have to

choose who not to choose.

Lucky Pennies Aint Shit

You know those days when nothing

goes your way?

Like having the money for your bills but

forgetting to pay.

Imagine rushing to pay in person but

the window closes and your next in line

Then finding out that your lateness

incurs a $50 fine

I realized that all of these things

happened ironically

The day that I stopped and picked up

A "lucky penny"

As I walked down the street,

I saw something shiny

I moved closer because the object was so tiny.

I was so excited because I didn't see many

I had come across

A lucky penny!

I naively picked it up

With expectations of

having good luck

And with confidence

into my pant pocket

I tucked.

But by the end of the day, I thought, Whoa! What The Fuck?

My day was better without it

I began to realize and admit.

I found out 1st hand that lucky pennies

aint shit.

I really didn't want to believe it.

I was in the first stage of denial and

not prepared to grieve it.

So the next day when I came across

A new lucky friend

I decided to have faith and try it again.

Surely this winning streak of

new found lucky pennies,

Was a sign that I was destined to win.

At least that's what I'd hoped the case would've been

but

It was not.

Everything that I learned from the 1st penny I forgot.

Had a good day with the new penny-

I did not!

I wondered if this was a crazy malfunctioning

lucky penny plot???

The thought of the penny being in my possession

had me nervous so

I stayed up all through

the night.

In fear of missing my

morning flight.

I was sleep deprived and half crazy

by day's light.

On my way inside the airport,

You know what I saw right?

Yeah, that copper devil heads up

In the 1 o'clock position

lied there

Right on the ground

I paused and looked at that shiny metal piece of shit up
and down

With a frown

Yet stood in the penny's time warp and pondered our
destiny

While in reality my flight was leaving without me

I had to reflect on luck

Either you have it

Or you don't

Walking around with a tiny copper puck -think it's going

to give you luck? It wont.

Besides I had come to the conclusion that I had no room
in the pockets of my outfit

Especially considering lucky pennies aint shit.

...but I did go back and grab it but

only because it's an extra 1 cent.

Seedless Fruit

To thine own self be true

despite all of the distracts

How can you decipher truth

wearing society's contacts?

Look into this mirror so that

The words can be seen clearer.

You are eating seedless fruit.

Don't laugh, it's not cute.

I hope this concept doesn't sound crazy that

your actions come across as lazy,

brainwashed and confused (just to name a few)

but

Tread lightly because

our youth

Are watching you.

When you hate yourself

you destroy your wealth

Stop reading fiction and

read about your health.

Work on it and

Don't deny it

Because your life is just as hybrid

As fruit made with no seed

But it's not your fault because you don't read

About the things that matter because you are too content
with having your Masters.

Consider treating yourself to a wholesome meal

Because Seedless Fruit

Is not REAL.

Rose Colored Shoes

Damn! You're so good. I've tried to find all the bad

things About you that I could

And the biggest thing I have come up with so far

Is that you don't even own a car.

You are a nice guy and you treat me just fine,

But I am just not attracted to your hairline.

So you wait here

I am putting my shoes on.

I am going to run and not walk seeking out Mr. Wrong.

Because Mr.Wrong gives me things to think about like,

Where is he at?

I lent him my car hours ago

He should definitely be back...

I think? #ShouldntHe?

Anyways, he motivates me to stay in shape by

Being honest and pointing out when I look fat.

There's a lot of competition out there

and I need to stay intact.

And You...You just love EVERYTHING

About me.

And for some weird reason all of my

Flaws you choose not to see.

Which equates to BORING... respectively

I need a reason for drama occasionally

So I'm putting my shoes on

To stroll down the street and

Hear about some blues.

I won't allow you to have me in the clouds.

That's not where I belong.

I don't get the happily ever afters

I've accepted I am destined for the sad love songs

The kind of love you offer is solid

Yet comes with no thrills

I deal with bad boys because they're aggressive and the sex kills

You are 1 in a million but my

Mr. Wrong is ALWAYS there.

He doesn't always treat me good

But hey! You can't have it all,

Life is not fair.

So I am putting my shoes on and I am

Tying the string TIGHT.

I can't keep Mr.Wrong waiting

He had to stand me up last night.

Ready Mind Heavy Heart

My mind is ready

But my heart

Is heavy.

From carrying the loads

No one else wants

To hold.

Unpoetic Poem

I write poetry

But I'm no poet

I love to love but afraid to show it.

I love to draw but have no passion

For art

Yet when the pencil is

On the paper

It's expressing

My heart.

I'm very emotional

But I won't shed

A tear.

Giving into myself Is my greatest

Fear.

Damn!

I am a contradiction of a contradiction!

My Soul is real but my life seems fiction.

I'm not a Poet

But I do love to

Rhyme

And read them aloud

From time to time.

Call me an Anti-Social Social Butterfly,

I will have to agree.

I know so many people

But they don't know me

I just create these life changing moments

very casually.

Then move down my uncharted path

very gradually.

Urgent Message

I feel a sense of Urgency

Burning deep inside of me.

Which way to go? Honestly…

I don't know.

Listening to myself

But the message comes slow.

So what is this fucking urgency

That calls for me to write this poetry?

Well, I recently had

A very clear vision.

That I am sick of making

Fucked up decisions.

I'm frustrated.

I look out the window

To the sun.

It tells me my work

Here is not close

to done.

So what is this rush of urgency

Trying to say that I just can't see?

O.K, I know that everything isn't always what it seems

But I saw myself happy and successful

In my dream

I talked to the moon and asked,

Could this future be true?

The moon replied

That everything is possible

Cause you're you.

Just be patient, take notes and enjoy

Your journey

Embrace the fire that's burning internally

More than anyone else love yourself

Mastering these

Understandings alone you

Will always have plenty of wealth.

And just remember that the feeling of urgency,

is you rushing you

to become free.

#freeme

Am I ready?

Am I ready to let you

Back in?

How do we start this over? Where to begin?

Can we start off pure

Even with a past?

We say we forgive,

But forgetting

Never lasts.

Am I ready to really let you go?

How much of my vulnerability

Am I willing to show?

I push you away only to look back

And make sure you are still there.

Yet when you ask if I want you to stay,

I shove it off as if I don't care.

I love you now.

I loved you then.

But am I ready

To let you

Back

In?

Never Ever

You are neeeeever ever getting

My love back.

I know you think that I'm

Joking.

But I'm not.

I will never trust you

With my love

Again.

Though I will eventually forget some things

Because the wounds will heal

I will always remember

The way you made me feel.

To make sure of that,

I have written myself

A little note that reads:

"DONT YOU EVER...

DONT YOU EVEN...

NO MEANS NO AND I'M PUTTING MY FOOT
DOWN.

DON'T CALL.

DON'T WRITE.

YOU WILL DISAPPEAR LIKE THE NIGHT.

YOU ARE NOT WORTHY OF MY LIGHT.

YOU ARE...NOTHING.

YOU ARE...ERASED."

I will read this letter 3 more times then place it

Back in the space that it came from.

Then do you know

What happens next?

Nothing.

Because, you will never ever Get My LOVE back

Again.

Pura Vida

Life is full of unexpected moments

Those moments come fast.

Life is your future

And Life is your past.

Something that most don't want to hold true

Is that life is something Bigger than you.

Life is great but when it's not good

Life can be hurtful

And so misunderstood

I've traveled through space

29

And they all ask why?

Is life a bitch and

Then you die?

The answer came to me and

it's very clear

Have faith through your rough days because

happiness is near

And take with you through all you

Endure.

Respect for change through the seasons

Because

Life is

pure.

The Gambler

I went to Vegas and lost it all.

I skipped the Strip avoided

Downtown.

And still left with nothing.

Though I avoided all of the things that

I thought would tempt me

I still left with my pockets

and my chest empty.

I left my heart vulnerable.

How did a person who didn't go

To any Casinos or slot machines

lose everything?

Well, I never said that I wasn't a Gambler.

I am actually the worst kind.

A high roller, the riskiest of them all

I gambled with my heart,

Then my car, house even shoes

In the end I turned to mush

I became the player that didn't know how to Lose.

I refused to call a fixed situation when I saw it.

I was the Gambler that would not accept their fate and

instead of taking the Loss

And going home

I attempted to win the losings back by

investing more into

My love for the favorite, his name was Blaze.

Oh I loved him so

and instead of betting on a one night stand

One taste and -

I said that I was all in.

I was in too deep it

sucked me dry but

I wanted so blindly

to take him off the board,

The move of a rookie

His moves were professionally calculated

Accepting illegal love bets for fun like a bookie

Las Vegas never promised me love

Its business lies in sin

He was sharp

I fell for his games

And would futures bet on him again

But *this* time with a wise guy wager

Because as they say

the house always wins

Fast Food Love

You've got that Fast Food

Kinda luv.

That short order quick

Service type shit.

"Hi, yes I'll take a NO.3

Love-On-the-run special ."

"Sir, would you like to add "savor-the-flavor"?

"No, that won't be necessary,

My order is done.

Oh---

But you can add on an extra

Honey bun."

You've got that ,"I want my food and I want it fast!" -

Kinda Luv

That Unhealthy shit

That stuff is no good for me but

I just can't quit-shit.

You've got that drive through luv.

No need to waste your time

taking out a plate:

I have no time for a dinner date

kinda luv.'

Fast food is convenient

I must agree

But I need you to order this special,

para aqui.

I'm afraid you don't meet the requirements so

elsewhere you should flow

Here's your NO.3, minus savor the flavor, plus extra

honey bun

To go.

Mind Trap

I'm trapped.

I'm trapped in a web

Of bad decisions.

But I now give myself

Permission to take a minute and

THINK BEFORE I ACT.

It's not a GAME!

Life won't let

You win your move back.

You'll have to face it-then own it

Hope that you survive it and

Come out stronger.

Don't allow your mind trap

To entangle your decisions any longer

Petty Nothings

Do you love me? Or do you not

You told me once

Then the loving stopped.

Outcast since birth

I was born with 12 fingers that were

cut off before I was 2

Yes, I was born with 12 fingers

It may sound weird and

Sci-fi but it's true.

When I say that I was born with 12 fingers

people ask what did the other 2 do?

Besides making me an Outcast and

becoming a part of me that I never knew

I cant answer that question honestly because

they were cut off moments after I was born.

So if later in life I have identity issues

Please excuse me because since birth

I've been torn.

Torn apart and sewed back together so that

I can fit the norm

But I have tried on society's cookie cutter

and never fit the form.

Doctors altered my appearance for vanity

and cut a couple of my

baby fingers off

yet

5 Finger gloves still don't

Fit me

They could cut off 'physical imperfections"

But not my unique personality.

What if my extra two fingers were a part of my security?

To keep away and scare off negative energy

People have said the fingers were removed

Because there was no function that they could do

But the truth in the answer is that,

They only removed my two fingers because

I was an Outcast and they wanted me

to look more like you.

Almost done

Is this the end of us?

Should we even try?

Is this the time

That we should say goodbye?

I do know this time when you left,

I didn't even cry

Though at night I held the pillow

Tightly with a sigh

F Love

Fuck Love!

And all of its Seasons

Want no parts in it

Regardless of the Reasons.

Questions ("Q" no "A")

I keep asking and wondering

How should love be?

Or...

Should I even want it

In a Loveless Society

I could live life nonchalant

But that wouldn't be me

Or...

Be a love sacrifice so that they

Can all see

To love is Divine and to feel it in return is

Even better

It does make you vulnerable

But it can also be your shelter

How does Love so easily

turn to hate?

Is having many loves

A part of our fate?

Or is it finding that one Love

And holding on for the ride

But...

Love sometimes bucks like a bull

And even if you aren't ready

Will toss you aside.

I'm a fool, a sucker, an addict of Love and

that's my confession.

Damn-I don't have any answers just

A whole lot of questions.

I can't help but to love love

It hurts but I can't quit.

Should I continue to love or

believe that it's just a bunch of bull shit.

I can't help but to ask because

I want to know the true essence

Of love

Is it a bite, a push and pull, should you fight or

sometimes a shove?

If you really want it, should you fight to stay?

If love dont want you, is it love

Or don't question it, just walk away.

If true love is out there I hope It finds me today

To love freely and not for

Convenience is the love

That I pray.

An Unconscious End

You are pushing me away without

Using your hands

Your words, your actions

Your unspoken demands

You are pushing me away

And I don't think that you understand...

The finality of your actions

Are bringing us to an end.

You are pushing me away with

Your hands behind your back.

The world is coming for us

But you remain slow to react.

You are pushing me away

With your pessimistic thoughts

They are manifesting in your life

Crowding the space where we should walk.

You are pushing me away.

Is that your intention?

Or a neglectful act to avoid Self improvement?

Q's Na A's 2

Why am I here?

What is my purpose?

Why make me think deep

While the masses

Are surface

Why have me here longing to be

struck by cupid

When everyone else thinks

That the "LOVE THING" is stupid

What is my purpose?

Why am I here?

With every year

They are bringing more fear

Most people are busy looking down

When the messages are up

85% are unconscious so why

Make me give a fuck

I sometimes feel alone because

They haven't realized

They're speaking empty words

The revolution won't be televised

You have to be 1 with self

And unfortunately there's

No app

They want us busy watching revolution videos

So that we are not out

Fighting back

But why do I know this?

Why am I chosen to have this information

Why make me live this life

When it's only an imitation?

Why make me so rebellious

When others are content

With formation?

It's so awful to relate

Happy times only

With vacation.

We want change! But don't

Know how to take the action

How can we when all of our attention has constant
distractions.

Am I just awaiting my ride and my ship is coming soon?

Do I keep wondering and praying

While looking to the moon.

Are there others out there struggling

To be the person you need to be

Is all of this confusion and chaos

What you need me to see

Please tell me my purpose so that I can feel free

Because what's the point of being conscious

If it's just me?

Get Out

From our conversation

you need to leave your relationship

And this is why

If you stay where your at

you're going to die

Not speaking in the sense of naturally but

Emotional, mental and/or physically

I understand The power of love, dick and pussy

But there will be plenty of that in your new reality

Minus the toxicity

You owe it to yourself

To be treated respectfully.

Its okay to get out now

And begin the healing.

Resident Madness

Am I mad?

Aren't we all mad here?

Trying to fix a puzzle

As the pieces disappear

Going through the madness

Appearing weak to shed a tear

Whatever vice helps me escape

is what I hold dear

Let me be clear

going mad I don't fear,

The judges of the masses are

crazier than they all appear

They have us racing towards a goal

That none of us are near

-and wont be

until we replace

money, media and material

With a spiritual tier.

Crazy is...

Crazy to think but it just hit me...

I never had a chance to spend a birthday with my ex.

The 1st year that we were together he blew me off because his friend surprised him with tickets to a Baseball Game-then stood him up.

The next year he broke up with me a few days before his birthday from what seemed like a "forced" fight.

He knew that I would keep putting up with his manic behavior and weekly break-ups

Because for his make ups

He would give me the world.

Initially, I thought these extravagant acts of forgiveness

showed just how much he loved me-

But

Then I realized that I needed to run because his ass was

actually just crazy.

Fuck Potential

Back when I was younger

I believed that potential

was something

that you could look forward to in a mate.

So upon meeting my future mistake

I convinced myself that he may not have his business

in order today but

the potential was clearly there.

I was so impressed with his future

I could see us growing into an ideal pair

So I moved forward building a union

with that mentality

but going after someone's potential

ended in a relationship fatality

Truth was, I wasn't pleased with his present state of mind

but I believed more than him sometime...

in his future self

And who he could be *potentially*

but I refused to face the reality

I was in love with a man that

he could but would never be

I began to look at him resentfully

I felt irritated that he ignored all of his potential-

why couldn't he see?

I responded with hesitation and handled

his dreams unnervingly

Helping him reach his potential made me

want to pull out my hair

I began to feel like he tricked me-

After all, not reaching his potential wasn't fair

I supported his struggles and like I said,

I did believe

but not in my man

only in the character that I wanted him to achieve.

Now I've learned to accept a person for their today and
give support in their growth

Embrace the qualities that you initially choose because
with Potential you just don't know.

#fuckpotential

Warrior Spirit

I have a lot to say

But who wants to hear it?

People see my pain and

don't want to go near it.

But when my strength shows

Most they fear it

The inner G is strong

in this Warrior Spirit

Petty Ending

Petty is conscious.

Petty is a choice

You may not be ready

For all of this petty

But I choose petty

As my voice

www.ingramcontent.com/pod-product-compliance
Lightning Source LLC
Chambersburg PA
CBHW021627270326
41931CB00008B/901